Judge Me Not
Without A Trial

By Dudley (CHRIS) Christian

A

Pause For Poetry ©

Publication

Acknowledgement:

Special thanks to my wife, Marilyn Christian for compiling, organizing and finalizing the books of my collections. Her photographing and editing skills were vital to all of my works.

ISBN: 978-0-9877501-1-2

First Edition January 2012
Revised Edition June 2017

Cover Photograph: Rainbow in Saskatchewan © Marilyn Christian

An Opening Word by the Author...

Many people often ask:

"How do you write and do you have to often rewrite your material?"

I have long summed up my answer to the above with the following:

"A Word, the written word, small purveyor of a thought, so like a thought, once thought, cannot be recalled, so too, a word once writ, should need NOT be re-written, for with such licence, we would but change ... the very substance of the thought."

... DNC © 1970

Dudley (Chris) Christian founded and hosted the first and only "PAUSE FOR POETRY" show dedicated solely to the introduction of new and unknown poets and their works. This TV series ran from 1974 to 1985.

Table of Contents

Dear Reader:

As a child in the Cayman Islands, I often visited the last bastion to slavery called Pedro's Castle, which now is proclaimed as an ex-pirate's Castle.

Though piracy may have been its use later, this castle was originally built by slaves belonging to the forefathers of at least one of the island's MLA representatives. Until the late 19th century's emancipation, Pedro's Castle was used as a slave castle.

My Grandfather told me that he was, in fact, born there. He was born free. Sadly, he found the body of the last Cayman runaway slave, Aaron, a friend from their boyhood days, at the Castle.

The first poem in this book, called "See... See" (page 1), will walk you through this Castle.

LOVE LIFTS US UP WHERE WE BELONG . . .

2004

1961

See... See

See that mound of rocks which formed a dividing wall
See those steps hewn from stone along that Castles wall
See those chains with rings set evenly apart
See that square room with thick walls
And exit at no part
See yet still the bones which the Sun has whitened now
See that piece of crockery
Which has been broken by the plow
See those beads someone hid within the walls
See that noose with the door
Below thru which they used to fall
Picture back a little to the days that used to be
When our forefathers lived as Slaves
To one day set us free
Can't you hear their crying
When from their loved ones they must go
Don't you think that for our freedom
They saw enough sorrow
Do you feel it right
That to us these days should come back
It seemeth so 'cause our rights
You've allowed to become slack
So clamp down on these people
Who would make us Slaves e'en still
And stand even as the old Slaves stood and died...
That we free might live.

Judge Me Not Without a Trial

Judge me not without a Trial

Condemn me not without a word

Take me not to yonder gallows

On the basis of what you've heard

Try me not when I'm not present

Give to me but freedoms right

Judge me not without a Trial

Tho I be Black and you be White...

Judge me not without a Trial

'Tis but Bigots that so act

Building fast through hate and ignorance

With vicious lies distorted facts

Living but with one ambition

As they go their ways along

Trying to keep down all others

Whether they be right or wrong

Judge me not without a Trial

As you slip out of my life

For in time too you'll be called

To take a stand for what is right

You'll be placed between two choices
Where lies and truth you'll know and then
You'll be asked for your own verdict
Black or White one choice my friend

Judge me not without a Trial
And as others so to me do
Keep yourself above their level
Find out first what's right and true
Judge me not without a Trial
Let your conscience be a guide
Then when their accusations falter
You still can look full in my eyes

Judge me not without a Trial
I who long have silent sat
While their hate has sought to lower
Every goal I've reached or sought
Judge me not without a Trial
Tho my skin's shade darker be
I was the stolen not the thief dear
I was the slave not an owner free
Judge me not without a Trial
And so soon you too will find
Their accusations proven falsehoods
As for my rights I stand this time.

Life is But a Story Told

Life is but a story told
Of lonely tales of woe
It holds its bright and pleasant times
And those laced by dark sorrow
We often strive to reach the top
But find we grasp but air
There's always someone there to stop
Our moving on elsewhere
Yet life is quite a teacher too
Of pain and love and grief
By its bitter disappointments friend
Convictions deep are reached
You'll see the ones you did respect
Proven false and ruthless too
The first time that you ask of them
The smallest thing to do
You'll see your life's work fade away
You'll feel the weight of loss
But with back bent you'll move along
To bear your every cross
For somewhere you have met or will
Find someone good and true
Who's worthy of the best of life
In all they think or do

So care not for this moment friend
When life's trials get you down
You've tried... and like the good seed you are
You'll grow beyond their bounds.

St John's Reversing Falls N.B.

O'er the hilltop I sat
Gazing at the waterfalls
As they went first this way then that
Those world famous "Reversing Falls"
The city below me it seems
So distant tho not far away
Like one in heavenly dreams
On the cool Canadian day
The river is no longer lazy
As many people would say
But it moves so softly and swiftly
To reverse a few times each day
I've longed waited to see such beauty
By which mine eyes would long stay
But to leave it soon is my duty
Else by the falls forever I'd stay
Just gazing from this lonely hilltop
As the river moves 'cross the bay.

~~ September 1963

Dreams of an Eight Year Old

Last night I lay upon my bed

In deep thought and rapture lost

Thinking of fine tables spread

With my peoples blood the cost

In my mind I chanced to gaze upon

With looks and thoughts serene

Exotic foods and lavish wines

Such as I'd never seen

A bird half carved, a piglet roast

A ham, a steak with pear

Imported fruits gold buttered toast

And finest Silver anywhere

A cloth of finest linen lay

Upon the tables top

While under every silver plate

A velvet red food sop

The chairs which did the places mark

Were of our craftsmen so unique

That the crimson and the black thereon

Did but compliment the teak

The curtains rich with valance hung

Free falling to the ground

With gold and red side sashes flung

To hold them to each bound

It seemed that I could taste the meal

Which was then being placed

So carefully upon each plate

By a skilled servant of my race

The kitchen door it was opened wide

And from therein I chanced

To gaze upon a black smiling face

By the meals splendour enhanced

Alas I reached to tell the host

That the meal was now 'Just right'

So quickly did he whip my hand

"No Black should touch a White"

I came back to reality

Gazed long my ragged bed upon

I am just eight a poor slave's son

God... How long can this go on???

Let Me Paint You

Let me paint of you a picture

As you rest upon my mind

As your recent form and figure

Stays warm in my thoughts and mind

Let me paint of you a picture

One which by I'll try to show

All that you in me awakens

Even tho far away you go

Let me paint of you a picture

Not in charcoals nor in oils

But in words which I'll remember

You best and all your toils

Let me look into the pictures

Of your secret distant thought

And from these lovely pictures

Let me paint a heart o'er wroth

Let me use not any canvas

Any cloth or wood or stone

That may serve to less encompass

The beauty that is yours alone

Let me use no brush or feather
Lest a stroke false once I make
And fearsome of losing you ever
Can't stop to 'move my small mistake

Let me paint of you a picture
As with hand on head you think
Of places you would like to be
Let me paint you with pen and ink
Let your eyes so bright and lonely
In the softest of green glow
Be the reaching point which only
Eyes alone like yours can show

Let me paint and thereby capture
With my pen your face so rare
Like a jewel which doth 'rapture
Costing men lives, loves and cares
Let me paint of you a picture
'Fore upon your ways you leave
Then in memories warm this picture
Will give me solace while I grieve.

I Wish You'd Taught Me Hate

I wish that in your teachings

From which I've learnt to read

From which I learnt about your past

Of your ancestors hate and greed

I wish that in your teachings

Where with figures great I work

Where sorrows and joyous memories

Bring laughter, tears or smirks

I wish that in your teachings

Which strove to bring me light

Which did their best to prove to me

Black is bad and good is white

I wish that in your teachings

Which I've studied until late

You'd taught me what you know so well

I wish you'd taught me hate.

I wish that in your teachings

Of God and love and life

Of peace and hope and freedom

Of living a good clean life

I wish that in your teachings

You had chanced to glance awhile

At me as man and taught to me

How to kill an infant's smile

I wish that in your teachings

Destruction, greed and hurt you'd shown

Then equipped now would I be

To rise and lead my own

If only in your teachings

You'd been honest fair and true

I'd be a heartless, ruthless man

I'd be white man... like you

I wish that in your teachings

We savages you took as Slaves

Had known love like yours for other men

'Stead of going quiet to early graves.

Paradise Memories...

On Caribbean waters

Where we drifted in the moonlight

I fell in love with you

The World seemed Paradise that night

On Caribbean waters

As we danced in the starlight

Your lips touched mine... the haze...

Around the moon seemed bright

One solemn kiss dear

Was fate that brought us first together

One glimpse of love Dear

That for us could never be

On Caribbean waters

As we wandered 'long the white sands

My heart did find a lifelong memory

Now Caribbean waters

Slowly lap upon the seashore

They move away those

Lines of love which once we knew

Oh Blue Caribbean waters

She is gone from me forevermore

She is gone... and I'm alone

Alone, alone once more with you.

Africa

Oh land so full of beauty

Which stretch from Sea to Sea

You hold the highest splendour

And home are you to me

Your white topped majestic mountains

Your creamy Coral sands

Your tall Black and stately peoples

Your forests oh so grand

Your mines of Diamonds, Gold and Silver

Your many tales untold

Your hard working populace

In awe the World doth hold

My great ancestors dwelt there

So happy prosperous free

Until they all were moved away

To be damned to Slavery

The backbone of Civilization

To the whole World you did show

Their cultures and their governments

From your examples did they grow

For trade, for peace, for freedom

For joy, for hope, for love

For pets, for animal helpers

For History... to you they move

They took your wealth and riches

They've killed your peoples free

They've desecrated all your Holy lands

And made a Slave of me

Yet, still we try with these peoples

Hoping they may human turn

Looking for our long lost rights

When God's love these people learn

From your Mediterranean borders

To your Cape pointing to the South

From your Gold Atlantic coastline

To where the Indian Ocean plays about

From deep within your chasms

Where your many riches lie

To your long and lovely rivers

By which your peoples die

From the tip-top of your mountains

To below your coral strands

My heart will long and ache for you

My home... My Fatherland

So Dearest Africa I salute you

With your varied coloureds all

For your endless patient waiting

For a return to what you've known

Oh Africa... My Homeland

Once happy and so free

You've held the secrets of all life

Yet life they've taken from me

Yet one day we'll enjoy friend

That land our fathers knew

Then Africa, My Africa...

I'll return once more to you.

A Tribute to Leilani

For ten years I have wandered

In search of just one dream

In the hope of one day holding near

The impossible it seemed

But one day my life was shattered

And my past was made anew

My dream it did materialize

That day that I met you

You were the answer to my hopes

A visioned girl so pure

You were the one I'd live on with

Of this my heart was sure

Yet tho you filled my hopes love

And helped my every scheme

There remained in me a memory

You had not filled... my dream

That dream was black and true dear

With brown base topped with red

With tiny tiny parts which would

Wind in love about my head

With an angel's song of heaven

With a sunshine gleam so bright

Bringing a rainbow's hope to me

Throughout each stormy night

Now love thanks to you I've found it

The answer to my dreams

I'm glad you realize it all so well

If my time there long doth seem

But you see the black hair, clear eyes

The brown complexion too

The lips so red the tiny arms

Remind me so much of you

Her voice is the angel's chorus

Her smile is sunshine bright

Her trust in me is plain to see

As rainbows before night

She is my dream and yet you gave

Her... in unselfish love so tender

To fill my life with peace and joy

You gave me this tiny daughter.

A Tribute to Beau

Shsss... there's a cry from out of a dream

The world and its woes around you appears

Then a hand tenderly touches you dear

Have no fear child your Daddy is here

Your Dad so young so careless and free

Is standing beside and watching you

If you cough or cry if you laugh or sigh

Have no fear child Daddy is near

I have no other reason to live

But to give unto one which to me God did give

A life as full as happy as free

As my daddy did once give unto me

My Dad is now old, weary and grey

With wrinkles all doffing his smiles

But his heart is as warm, his love is as strong

As on those nights when like you I'd squirm

My dreams were oft troubled my son just like you

By things which have now long gone past

But I knew it was all right with my Daddy too

When I reached out and held his hand fast

So sleep on sweet child of tomorrow

You've brought joy to your Mommy and I

And when you are grown

'Twill be nice to have known

Your Daddy was there standing by

As you grow my son and life greets you

Your Dad soon may pass on his way

Yet unseen... tho not unknown

You need ne'er fear for someone watches o'er you

There's a Daddy up above us in Heaven

He's the best of the Daddies of all

He loves one and all helps you if you fall

And He watches wherever you go

So... have no fear child if when you're awakened

Tho the night it be dark and drear

For as long as I can I'll remain by your side

But forever God your great Daddy is near...

Vancouver... City of Splendour

Vancouver... city of splendour
Which sleeps at night so calm
With star-like lights you twinkle
Keeping your treasures safe from harm
Your trees and hills and rivers
You let flow and freely run
You've learnt to live everyday
But sleeps at set of sun
Yet city of such riches
Your greatest beauty lies
Not in your gold or silver
But shining from your skies
The glow of starlights twinkle
The bright new moon above
These bring joy to hearts all broken
These speak of peace and hope and love
But have you ever noticed
Those simple things above... Nay...
You work towards their end
With your egotistical love
Pollution from your factories
Pollution from your cars
Pollution from your industries
These do the night skies mar

'Till now no longer star nor moon
Be visible here below
You'll seek too late to find the moon
But its peace you'll ne'er 'gain know.

What is a Conscience

What is a conscience
What is guilt
What is their crime
What is the reasonings
What places and what times
What peoples are we
What wrongs have been done
What should be their punishment
What group or which one
What proof of these doings
What right them to judge
What hope for our futures
What now is our plan
What tells of their guilt
What now to let us free live
We their consciences
We Unfreed Black Slaves

Earth's Mortal Song

If you but have a moment friend

To go my way along

I'd like you to come listen in

To pain... Earth's Mortal song

I'd like to take your hand in mine

And show you where I've tread

I'd like to share life's other side

Here along with these living dead

I will not, cannot, should not name

The places we'll pass thru

But in the mind you'll feel the pain

Of disgust strike out at you

You'll see the rows of houses stacked

As if against a leaning wall

You'll see the roaches and the rats

From sewer to kitchen crawl

You'll see the young and innocent

Being raped and mugged and beat

You'll see the laws of justice spent

And these living dead ill-treat

You'll try to breathe the stinking air

Which is filled of sickly smell

You'll walk thru garbage everywhere

See filth high where humans dwell

You'll look at me and wonder deep

Why neither word or move I give

Standing steadfast like in dreary sleep

You'll see friend where I live

I live here in among the dirt

The filth and garbage hills

In these tenements which you condemned

But left for my kind to fill

You'll look alas and wonder what

Can bring back to life what's lost

Equality is but a little thing

But we can't afford its costs

I too am what you may not know

A Black Man... a Human Being

Condemned to live in this ghetto

While in luxury you are living.

I the Slave Remembers

What do you know of pain or hurt

Why are you so afraid

I've lived and hurt bled and loved

In a thousand different ways

I've known the pain of hunger deep

I've known the hurt of hate

I've known the toil of haunted sleep

I've known the curse of fate

I've seen the gallows and the sea

As convict and as Slave

I've tried many tortures that be

I've rotted without a grave

I've seen my children in their youth

Die of torture every night

I've seen my parents for the truth

Lose life and limb and sight

I've felt the pull of heavy chains

Upon my legs and arms

I've seen innards of brothers lain

On streets for freedoms alarm

I've been a cripple and a slave

I've been many men's revenge

I've lived in holes and shallow caves

Awaiting their sweet revenge

But lastly I have been to some

Who now suffer still again

The hope and strength of days to come

I've been to man a friend

So if I hurt you in my time

I'm sorry friend it's true

To keep you happy at all times

Is but all I did intend to do.

> Momma said, "*Discipline:*
> *upside your head, or 'cross your butt*
> *keep you outa jail in later life.*"

Hold Fast

Hold fast

Hold fast little one

I hear you calling

So distant yet distinct

I hear your voice

I know it's you that I hear calling

But I wonder at the pain that's in your voice

I've never known you little one to cry

I've ne'er e'en li'l one heard you sigh

Yet I've heard the music so often

That I know it's your voice that I hear calling

You grew here sheltered and protected

You of the woes and sorrows never knew

The World, its hates and prejudices

I've tried li'l one to keep from you

Still alas across the way I hear you

I hear you calling now... as if in pain

I wonder if the world has finally found you

And will it instill within you grief and pain

Oh little one I am delayed here

By bars and chains I can't release

By hate and prejudices of the bigots

Who seek to stay our race's increase

Oh little one you're so finely fashioned

From the softest of the velvet black I've seen

Now like a lamb innocent you're led to slaughter

Condemned by their prejudicial scheme

No tongue can tell the pain we suffer

No words on paper can the truth unveil

No laws will stand to stay our daily trials

They've e'en painted white our God our Shield

So hold fast little one

I hear you calling

So distant yet distinct I know your voice

Stand tall and firm on your convictions

Let Equality and Freedom be your only choice.

Why Why Can't I Live

Take my hand... touch it

Is it so different from yours

If it isn't... then why can't I live

Touch the hair on my head... feel it

Is it so different cause of its curls

If it isn't then why can't I live

Look in my eyes... search deep

Are they dead, cold and unseeing

If they aren't then why can't I live

Reach over now here... Kiss my lips

Do they feel inhuman or weak

If they didn't then why can't I live

Why... oh why... why can't I live

Why can't the life that you treasure

And all of the things you desire

And all the rights you enjoy

And all of the laughter you know

Be a part of this hard life of mine

Why can I share in your work

Share in your everyday bills

Cry thru the nights alone

Know pain and sorrow my own

Know want and hunger and hate

Yet see you pass by me each day

Tho so much alike we are made

Why, oh why... why can't I live

Why can't my heart beat anew

Filled with love and freedom like you

Ne'er turning 'round asking what I lack

Not needing to fear when I turn my back

Free to live on life's other track

Free to live like you tho I'm Black

Oh why... why... why can't you let me live?

The Artist Has Settled

The artist has settled in comfort

To paint him a picture so bright

He's settled with paint and with brushes

But his subject is far from his sight

Uplooking he sees but a pinpoint

Of beautiful soft yellow light gleam

And he wonders if ever that beauty

Could be captured by him as it's seen

Taking a soft black piece of velvet

And stretching its beauty nearby

He daubs in the oils and looks upwards

To the soft yellowy light in the sky

He notices that it is pulsating

Sending near it both orange and green

Which extends to surround and expand it

And to brighten its goldish bright sheen

'Tis but a star he views with such pleasure

As with eyes practiced and clear he tries

To on his velvet capture this treasure

Gleaming so bright from the skies

The face upwards held fast is unmoving

As with fingers his brush scurry on

As through his eyes and fingers he's creating

A transformation... that velvet upon

See the clouds in place slowly enter

'Til the stars seems to 'ave leapt from above

As the velvet becomes the heavens he's under

And the star is transported with love

Ah; at last he has broken his upglance

Looks down on his creation with pride

With a thank you for being given this one chance

He caresses his picture and cries

He's a Artist sure fully and honest

One who knows that his talent was given

Not created nor learned nor adapted

But beyond that star sent down from heaven.

A Part of God...

I am but a part of God...

I guess you feel that way too

But did you ever stop to realize

God made the light and dark

Before He made me and you

Do you ever watch the sea

On a moonlit night

Don't you wonder at the beauty

Of waves with moonlight shining bright

Don't you wish that you were pure

And could go so far away

Or do you get beneath a cloud

And gaze at the dark side of the bay

I feel that when God planned this earth

He made it all this way

The moonlight showed His love for us

The dark side... for those who went astray

He said that if we each would do our best

To do what's right each day

And welcome in our hearts His love

Our dark 'twould fade away.

Life's Other Side

My child is looking at a picture

While just a-standing there

Of a young and happy man

Of a maiden oh so fair

Of dreams in the making

Of a lifetime just begun

Of hopes of a love forever

Shared with no other one

Of children laughing, playing

Of sorrows and of joys

But ah, alas we failed to look

At life's other side

Looking at that child of two

Standing so forlorn

He really looks a lot like you

He really needs a home

He reaches up and touches light

The picture there with pride

And wonders who was really right

Looking at life's other side

He reaches up again and says

Most to himself a prayer

"Da-de Da-de" and wipes away

The trickle of a tear

He goes up and embraces warm

Mother sitting lonely there

And wonders if his Daddy will

Be coming back home again

Alas he looks and waits in vain

For the thing that makes him cry inside

For his Dad is gone forevermore

There to life's other side

His Dad is gone to set free

His Mother's wandering thoughts

To help her find herself somehow

And remove the grief he'd brought

He's gone to seek a life that's real

Where lonely fathers go

To where their little girls and boys

No longer can them know

To where lost men with broken hearts

With broken bodies, spirits too

Seek fellowship with those like themselves

Who've done all they could do

To where a lonely pair of arms

May someday make them men again

To where the pride of manhood grows

'Til tall they'll stand again

To where the bottle and the street

Is their home their joy their pride

And loneliness their lifelong mate

There on life's other side...

Why Change You Us...

Oh men of might and power

You spend your every day

In books deep to discover

How to kill in different ways

You take your lands resources

To build your weapon toys

To maim to kill to conquer

You force your teenage boys

You've no heart for humanity

You've no feelings 'tis plain to see

You've no courage to live in harmony

You've no thought but to destroy me

Peoples have lived years in freedom

'Mong lands and thru ages past

In peace and health and harmony

But you came and it couldn't last

You brought the might and money

You brought power and your overkill

You brought hatred to my simple people

Oh killers why try to change our will?

Thoughts of a Woman

You say to love you is to trust

You say to love you is to have patience

You say to love you is to be lenient

You say to love you is to understand

Honey my trust is limited

I can only trust what I see

To trust what I hear my mind warps and misconcepts

Patience... with that I was endowed

But it wears thin relying on memories of your kiss

Or in waiting for your return

I realize you are spoken for

Yet I dream... soon you'll be free

Free to love and make love only to me

I try and understand...

Our moments together are precious

Yet...

They do not last long enough for me

To fully express my feelings

To love me is impossible...

I take... for my body demands it...

I give... because in order to take I must give

I want you all the time...

Day and night... morning and afternoon

Yet...

I want to be free... for what I do not know

To feel a woman... that you gave to me
Will it go when I say goodbye to you
You taught me to speak... not of stars and sky
But of hurts and joys... will that go too?
How can I want you yet leave you at the same time
Is that love... I have no answers only questions
My feelings are real... my heart knows the truth
Yet...
My mind reasons, fights and
Eventually overpowers my heart
I am afraid to trust my heart
My heart desires love close
Yet not necessarily physical love
Just comfort and security...
Can you give that to me???
Physical love is not a median
By which I can express my feelings or desire
Yet...
With you my feelings are tripled
My heart rushes with yearnings for your touch
Is that the basis for our love?
Is it an ego trip for you?
Something to jest and laugh at... ?
My heart cannot believe this...
Yet my mind asks...
When you are not near me

My heart is burdened with questions
My mind throws at it
When you are close...
My heart rejoices and yells at my mind...
"You are full of Bull"... but really is it... ?
Am I nothing more than a pleasant and
Easy time killer for you... ?
Filling empty moments between work and home...
for you... ?
Will you say what a mixed-up chick I am
and laugh your heart out???
Or will you try and answer my questions
As you walk out the door
For the last time... ?
Will you assure my feelings and
Thereby strengthen our relationship
No matter what your decision... ?
I thank you for your patience...
If what I feel for you is worth saving
It is only because you feel the same
That is enough for me...
You taught me to understand...
You taught me to trust...
You gave me my womanhood...
My gratitude to you will never fade...
Nor will my heart ever forget you...

Strangers Arms Awaiting

Daddy... Daddy... Daddy...

Cries a little girl and boy

Each day and night with Mommy

Alone she they enjoy

Yet somewhere living sorry

For the mistakes he has made

Lives the man who is their Daddy

'Cause here's the price he paid

He lost his son and daughter

He lost his love and wife

He lost his joy and laughter

He lost his happy life

He lost his home and warmth

He lost his livelihood

He lost the one he left them for

Because she was no good

She took him in the shadows

Caressed him with practiced arms

With painted lips she let him go

In surrender to her wanton charms

She promised him blue heavens

And more milk and honey days

With nights so full of warmth and love

And that she'd never stray

When she had taken all he loved

Possessed his heart and soul

She traded then his love and trust

For cold and evil gold

She laid a trap ah he was caught fast

A victim of the plot

He's paid his price for extra love

Aren't you proud of what you've got.

Set Us Free to Live

Well it's that time again my love

My heart fills and calls in vain

My hopes run high and die in pain

Looking for a change of life

Why must wars go on and on

Why must all our young be killed

How long till the guns are stilled

How many graves must be filled

By hate and greed and power

Oh voice that cries out for our lives

That fills our ears with all your lies

That says it's for the good that our young dies

Answer now our pleas

Answer now and tell us true

What right to kill and maim have you

What Holy cause we fight for pray

Not Freedom?? Ours you've taken away

Your wars have claimed our cream of youth

Dying for your great untruth

Oh Liar since you answer not

Then set us free to live.

Now You've Finally Taught Me Hate

Not many years ago I recollect

When first to this place I came

I held respect for many things

Called I no one by slurred name

I stood at times alone and lost

At times with friends as man

Full equal free I thought I was

Racism I did not understand

I'd heard of hate, prejudice, Bigots

Other slurs and terms at times

They were but words by others used

I thought no use for them I'd find

I held the thoughts that brothers violent

Used these to retaliate

Against the ones who did them wrong

I had not learnt to hate.

Aye, yes but that was years ago

Six... Seven I'm not sure

For slowly... slowly you've filled me up

Of righteous anger with no cure

You've taken all out of my life

'Til barren I must stand

And still you seek to take e'en now

These feet from a poor Black Man

In subtle ways you've worn me down

You all my laughter in ways killed

My pride, respect and hope for life

With doubt, fear and despair you've filled

So now at last I've come to see

Pray I now that it's not too late

My last lesson from you I've learnt

At last you've taught me hate.

Hate is but an opposite

To the love and joy I've felt

Hate is but a violent act

In answer to the pain one's dealth

Hate is living by the rule

Of doing others e'en as they've done

Hate is putting down the writing pen

And taking up both sword and gun

Hate is being able once more to live

With my human pride intact

Hate is making sure revenge to deal

To answer every hurt-filled act

Hate is a feeling deep within

Which casts our reason aside

It eats at you both day and night

To release the animal from inside

So long I've lived in peace content

Wish it could have stayed that way

White man why did you push so long so hard

To teach me to hate now this way??

Let the Day Begin

Let the day begin

Let the day begin

Let the birds sing sweet refrain

Let the day begin

Let man find his worth

Let peace reign on Earth

Let freedom be theirs at birth

Let the day begin

Let us live and laugh and shout

Let the feelings suppressed out

Let there be joy and love about

As the day begins

Why... why... why... ? why not?

Soon enough the day will end

Soon the Sun will set again

Soon the birds will stop refrain

Soon the day will surely end

Soon the day will end

Too soon man will have no worth

Too soon peace will leave the Earth

Freedom 'twill be taken at our birth

As the nighttime settles in

As the nighttime settles in

No more will we recall

The laughter, joy we suppress all

The love we'll crave we won't find

As the day begins to end

Oh friend or foe hear now my plea

The day you live 'twas lived by me

Now in the night I live unfree

There's nothing left at all for me

I cannot live, love or be free

My day is gone... my day is gone

My night has come.

Ah I Was the Victim...

A woman white and well learnt

I spoke to by chance one day

We talked awhile and then she did

On me this question lay

Do you think the Black Man

In all that he may do

Will ever rise up to be equal

With the White Man, do you?

I stopped and laughed tho steaming

For such ignorance to find

I had not thought still possible

From such a well read of her kind

Then slowly I gave answer

That fully each word she'd understand

I was the stolen not the thief friend

I started out above the man

It took awhile to settle in

Her closed and tiny mind

Then at me she looked in deepest hate

Yet no reply now could she find

In awkward silence she stood there

As I explained the thoughts of mine

I told her that a victim dead

Is not to a trial sent
But rather he who the victim made
Is for his guilt by the law bent
It is not on the fire strong
That the insurance lays the blame
Put the arsonist who did start it all
The real cause of the flame
At times in life it happens tho
That right is kept e'er down
Whilst wrong is the exalted one
Like these lives of yours and mine
Thus friend you should be wary
When questions such you ask
For what you often misunderstand
Will bring you to dreary task
So I repeat again to you
The Black will never rise
For to equal with the White man be
The Black he must backslide
She spoke no more in answer
She hung her head and then
Slowly walked away without a word
I wonder if she's still a friend.

Four Years Old...

It was on the M. V. Nanaimo
One sunny eve this Spring
I chanced to gaze my eyes upon
A most sweet and darling thing
So tiny and so tender
So pure with head all a-curl
My eyes did chance to stay upon
A nice and lovely girl
She sat so trim and proper
In her chair for all to see
With cheeks red as the roses
And eyes blue as could be
To match her eyes and dress too
Which quite short and frilled she wore
In her hair a barrette sky blue
Which pleased me even more
Her lips like rose buds puckered
With a dimple on each cheek
Brought to me thoughts remembered
Of which I seldom speak
And as the ship sailed onwards
O'er the sea and the tide
I felt that I would love to have
Her right here by my side
But alas I know it just can't be
Tho to her my heart is gone

She belongs to someone else you see
With whom she must travel on
Yet one day in our travels far
I hope once again to behold
That beautiful little blonde haired child
Who's only Four Years Old...

Mr. President

The White House
Washington, D. C., U.S.A.
Dear Mr. President,
You tore up our home when he left me
On your orders he flew 'cross the seas
Now you've sent me three Vietnam Medals
But here Sir, they're no good to me.
So... Golden... Bronzed and Silvered
A packet to you I return
May they help to bring you forgiveness
May they help Sir your soul not to burn
My life was once quite contented
My children a Daddy once knew
Now we live in the ghetto on welfare
And yes Sir it's all 'cause of you.
You've taken our men by the thousand
To fight in a strange foreign land
Still at home we know of no freedom
And for their lives you send a Blue Velvet Band...

The Tanker...

Low in the sea she lay

Like a waterlogged angel

Silently speeds on her way

That giant of cold iron

So like a babe she seems

In loving arms cradled

So safe snug secure from harm

For as long as she's stable

Oh but alas there comes

From deep deep down under

Wavelets that giants turn

To toss and to pound her

Now up on Oceans crest

Now deep deep down she flounders

Still again once more to rise

In beauty and in splendour

So high atop the waves

She climbs and there she resteth

'Til time to bow down again

In the next wave that cresteth

Ah but to feel again

The joy the love and dangers

As over the seas we float

In some sure bottomed tanker

The schooners may come and go

The yacht pitch and ponder

The cruiser may speed on top

Whilst the sub lumbers under

Yet tho they all may woo the sea

Or ride on the swelling tide

A tanker... home will always be

To any seaman of salty pride.

Tribute to the BC Ferries Catering

I've so often thought and wondered

As at my work I strove

What makes the peoples near at hand

Seem so mean so hard so cold

They never seem to know to say

For service they receive

The slightest thank you in a way

That the poor worker can believe

It seems they think we workers all

Are mere paid servants for their use

To rush and curse and needless call

For further of their abuse

Yet if they'd stop a minute now

To realize their mistake

They too would soon ponder how

Their thankless patronage we take

They're patrons of our employer yes

And for this we're truly grateful

But their patronage is his at best

And our wage but only livable

We're up at early morning dark

Some tune in their car radios

To listen 'til they reach the park

To the four or five AM hillbilly show

Then for ten long and lonely hours

A smile 'twill bright their faces

As thru hail or snow sun or showers

They attend their many places

A hand burnt or an order changed

They take with jolly gesture

They've oh long learnt to full control

Their thoughts their tongues and temper

And even thru the holidays

They may drink but still remember

That ne'er can an excuse they say

To cover any blunders

But will apologize as is their way

And soon rectify their actions

Yet at each day's end you will see

The patrons have most forgotten

To leave a bit of gratuity

For the worker who did serve him

And counting out the few they get

One thing stands out unhollered

Gratuity is shown in cents as yet

As lesser grows the dollar

So friend or stranger and patron all

If this you've chanced to read

Remember we're underpaid all

And really are in need

So next time that you pass our way

Be not one like the others

Don't STIFF your waiter friend today

Leave a TIP... Blessings he'll mutter...

A Letter to Mother

Dearest Mother when you read this

It will be far past the time

Any aid to me to render

Save bury these few bones of mine

You'll find me here upon the street

Not too far from where I grew

Where tomorrow's morn when I meet whitey

I'll do that which I must do

I've never meant to hurt you Mom

I've loved and respected you and Dad

I haven't from the true way turned

But I'm sick of hate so bad

You two no finer souls there be

This Earth's face to walk upon

I've seen what is meant to be

If within whitey's rule I go on

You may recall my younger days

When I would get into fights

Coming home scarred face broken bones

Thinking to be beat by him's alright

Now I've grown to be too old Mom

To lead on my life this way

No more a boy to be kicked around

Mom, I must make my stand today

There are so many good Black men Mom

Who feel the same as I

We know now that for some free to live

There must be some willing to die

I've done all that I've wanted to

While I've walked upon this land

Except to walk in freedom sweet

Equal to every other man

Alas Dear Mom it seems this way

Is all that's left now to try

I'm not afraid it must be done

I'm willing Mom for them to die

Again to you and Dad I say

Thank you both for all you've given

We'll meet again equal free one day

With our multicoloured God in heaven.

Man's Fantasies

See the beauty which the eyes give

When a man woman goes by

See the eyes from head to feet

Gaze and linger near the thigh

See the measurements all taken

Into brain and multiplied

As the thoughts of memories quicken

Reviving things he thought had died

Now she moves to yonder bench

In the park across from him

There she stops then slowly sits

Knowing she's being watched by him

For a glancing moment only

Doth her upper bare thigh show

But he misses not the beauty

From which now fantasies he'll grow

Looking upwards, side and backwards

She extends her neck so slight

Causing as her lax arms resteth

Sweater thin to be pulled tight

Up towards her neck he looks long

Slowly dropping eyes 'til they

Rest her firm uppointed breasts upon

Where his eyes linger and stay

Then a twitch of muscle tells him

That her comfort now must change

As he sees her full legs long slim

Slowly move to be re-arranged

Down upon her 'gain his eyes go

Down to knee and welcome thigh

Waiting for her changing moments

Once again warmed through his eye

Ah the moment sought approaches

Yet she slips her legs but slight

As so cunningly she crosses

Left o'er right and out of sight

Ah the beauty which eyes summon

As in dreams man life renews

With each new warm feminine woman

Tho but one from life he'll choose...

The Wind

Without a murmur, whisper sound

Without a thing to see

Without a trace of where it's been

Left on land, or sky or sea

Without a moments hesitance

Without a care or cause

Without a pressure or a push

Without hurry or a pause

Without a colour that we all

Could look to see again

Without a fragrance faint that lingers

Comes and goes ever... the Wind

We know it's here... we feel it

We know it's gone... sometime

We know it's needed too

To sustain lives like yours and mine

Yet tho so filled and heavy

It floats so softly by

And tho so precious yet to life

Can't contain it tho we try

Where did it come from in the past

What made its properties right

To sustain life and let pass thru

Cold, warmth and bright Sunlight

If nature did by a slight mistake

This wind we know create

How long will it be 'fore nature

Changes it and so our fate

We can't survive or so we're told

Without this invisible being

Which fills and enters everywhere

Yet eludes all our entrappings

And lastly now below the tides

Where trees grow and fishes wander

Thru waters calm or waters deep

You enter even there under

You give me life you give me love

You fascinate and awe me

Oh wind or air or demon still

Pray never e'er forsake me...

Tribute to Chief Dan George

Oh great man that thou art

You whose skin the Gods did hue

You whose peoples taught the arts

To those who then massacred you

You whose brow upon is writ

In marks of ages past and time

The pains you bore with true grit

'Til tranquility and peace you'd find

Oh Chief so great and noble

So outstanding are you 'mongst men

Tho your peoples may ne'er be able

To rise as free Indian men again

You once knew the taste of conquest

You did bare the losers pain

But with them all you still stand best

To forgive and live and try again

May that great and patient father

Whom you one day soon may meet

Take you to His tribe forever

Where you'll ne'er again know defeat

But 'til then may all your wishes

For your peoples all come true

'Til on this their land their smallest wishes

Of equal freedom they share too

And Dan George you mighty Chieftain

All your people will live in pride

Proud of their heritages all as Indians

Proud of ancestors brave who died.

True Beauty

What is true beauty... true beauty

The kind that every man seeks

The kind every woman craves

The kind that pleases our fancies

From our youth unto our graves

True beauty has many forms dear

For to the beholder it is the beheld

The one or the thing that appeases

The object on which deep thoughts dwell

It's to the driver the auto he's driven

Which has brought him pleasure full store

To the mason it's the artwork completed

Into which he's placed his soul

To the artist it's the oil on the canvas

Which has brought full worldly acclaim

To the politician it's the promises given

Which has pushed him to power and fame

To the infant it's the warm love of mother

As to a breast tender it is placed

To the convict it's the legal jury

Which his sentence at last has erased

To the teacher it's the grades of the pupil

Who has gone from bottom to top

To the actor it's the wonder of filmstrip

Which elates him with every prop

To the vain woman it's the feeling of vanity

Completed in spite of all costs

To the heartbroken it's the picture hidden

Of the love that was once known and lost

Yes to so many true beauty is varied

By the things they see, feel and do

But true beauty to me is true love dear

That's why true beauty to me Love is YOU...

A Heart and a Man

You say he's left you all alone

And you can't reason why

You're broken up because he's gone

You so often sit and cry

Your heart is full

You say that you

Just can't believe it's true

You'll never understand you say

Why he walked out on you

But baby... a heart and a man

Both are constant

Neither from sweet warmth will go

But a heart and a man

Can't be faithful

When there's nothing

To be faithful to...

He left you for some other woman

Who shares what you wouldn't give

One who knows how to be a full woman

One who likes to love and to live

No in his heart he wasn't fickle

But the truth is you didn't respond

So he's left now to live life a little

With a woman that he can count on

Maybe one day you will meet love

Love that is shared also by you

Then you'll find a man e'er near love

As you respond to all he may do

You will find then that you are a woman

Nothing greater in life could you be

When that happens then no other woman

Will see the emptiness she saw in me.

Forever Hold Your Peace

Crushed, broken, torn asunder

How cruel the world seems today

Alone, lost, friendless and crying

You thought you'd ne'er see this day

Cursed, jailed, rejected and accused

For the joy you did try to give

Oh love where is thy warmth now

Oh death show me your sting

Life is so useless and empty

Words are all so hollow and cold

Each day's sunrise has no meaning

My nights are still, dark, dismal all

Why has the light flown from me

Why shun I the coming of day

Why ask now for death's presence

To take me forever away

Alas friend so kindly you wonder

So I'll tell in a few words to you

How the world is built from one centre

How I lost that centre so true

My life and my love and my hopes friend

Were centered around just one heart

She loved me and gave me contentment

She was true to me at the start

But alas her eyes they were blinded

And she's left now taking my life

She's happy I hope and contented

In the role she has now choose to play

But friend as you're married tomorrow

Think of my wife that you stole away.

Homesickness...

From green green grass to smoky mountains
From railroad tracks among the trees
Even tho I feel a bit at home here
I long to be back in the West Indies.
"We've got no rivers with long long bridges
We've got no ferries for an evening ride
We've got no chimneys that's tall 'n' smoky
Nor hills with a white and icy side
We've got no trains that chug and whistle
We've got no mills with their clack, clack, clack
We've got no armed planes with their droning
And yet I'm longing to go back"

Oh back at home to me is lovely
Oh back at home we all are free
We live by the Golden Rule and morals
And love our neighbours with sincerity
But... but... but...
We've got a sea that's clear as crystal
We've miles of sand like fresh fallen snow
We love our land which God did give us
And all the creatures He did put below
There's no one there who talks of races
There's no talk there of Kith or Kin
We're everyone there to the other equal
And no one's judge by his native skin

The Clouds...

Like another land afar

Floating grey and white so high

Constant as we hurry on

Content to float the expanse of sky

Like a powdered cotton field

That's been picked and ruffled all

Into a picker's huge huge bag

Only to thru the bottom fall

Bits of black and bits of grey

Spotted here and intertwined

With the powder white and grey

Which seems to be a base of thine

Clouds... what mystery you hold

As you float o'er all on high

Now in bits and pieces broken

Now in mass you pass us by

Here a tiny isle you form

There a chain of mountains tall

Here a ladder to you clouds to the sky

There a fountain in cascades fall

Sweet and cool and so refreshing

Water to our lands you give

Or the floods cause and the snow

To stamp out the lives we live

Then returning in your beauty

To your innocence pure and white

Lending shade from Summer's sun

Changing moonglow in the night

Floating, floating ever onwards

Ne'er twice the same scene to portray

Changing, changing ever changing

You hold my interest Clouds... each day...

Calling to You...

Imaginings of you

As raindrops glisten from the rooftops

Imaginings of you, Imaginings of you

As teardrops drown my joy

Imaginings of how I would make you happy

Imaginings of you, Imaginings of you

Imaginings of how you'd return it too

Imaginings of love, comfort, consolation

Imaginings of you, Imaginings of you

Torment my empty soul

In it is a vacant hole

Imaginings of a warm embrace, soft kiss

Wholeness in one

Imaginings of soft breezes,

warm sun and beautiful sunsets

Imaginings of my life with you my love

Imaginings of you... and me...

Imaginings of you...

Dedicated to my family and all of the friends and to those who have worked to help our cause and quest for equality and freedom, with deepest gratitude.

My Friend "Les"

You've been to me an honest man
In valour warm and true
You've done your best in all you can
To stay a true friend too
When lands and country held me down
You outstretched to me your hand
You must have felt the pains I borne
Still you were a friend to man
Your travels now will take you far
Perhaps out of our days
But I'll recall wherever you are
Your genuine straight ways
And maybe once somewhere in time
We'll chance yet to meet again
'Til then and always warm in mind
You'll stay as a true friend
So should your travels ever lead
To places you would see
I hope if you're e'er in need
You won't fail to call on me
'Til time passes
And our path crosses
May Health, God and Luck
Be your constant companions.

Reflections...

Reflections are but visions
Brought to eye or mind
Of days and times long gone on
Or things we'd hoped to find
Or yet perhaps a memory
Of joy, or pain or sorrow
Which still our hearts doth cherish
For many a drearer tomorrow
Thus friend here in these verses
I'll try to bring to you
A few of life's reflections
As given to me by you
A stranger and a traveler
My life didst bid me stay
Awhile here in your city
E'er I passed on my way
In ways you did reject me
In ways you've left me stunned
But still I wish to share again
These little things I've learned
At last my thoughts do wander
To the far off Tropic Seas
Where long ago you came and met
My home, my life and me
And tho my Reflections vary
As land to land I pass by
May you see herein that part of me
Which equates friend you and I.

There Was an African

There was an African

Who had known no change

He stayed free and content

To walk along Afric's seashore gathering shells

He heard a sudden strange confusing noise

Looked up and stood frozen in fear

For on the seas where nothing was before

Moved thereo'er hugh ships

With golden sunlit sails

With masts like poles

And on they bore

And he in fear

A naked Black alone

His trembling hands

Forgetful of their shells

His knees like liquid

Force him low behind a stone

Therefrom to stare and see

But yet not to understand

John Hawkins slave-seeking British-ships

Slant to the shores

And the wretched slavers' land

Footnote: Acknowledgement with gratitude to
Sir John Squire for "There was an Indian"

Life is the Essence...

Life holds a shaky hand

It is the hand of aged Father Time

You wonder why the years roll on

But you never stop to really find

That life is the essence of all

Life is the essence of all

The good, bad or indifferences you've known

Life is the instigator of all

That to you at anytime befalls

Life makes you whatever you seem

It's the fulfillment of each dream

That clears your thoughts or mind

Yes, life is the essence of our time

Time is the owner of that shaky hand

The aged servant which doth before you stand

In mockery, in want or else in shame

'Cause forever he'll remain the same

But you dear are the thing that is

You are the existence of that thing

Which claims and which controls

Both life and time itself... you are

Taking both in stride... you go

Or yet returning empty-handed and alone

With but the memory of your lifetime

But alas no essence at all of life

Or of the times gone on you've known

Why... why... why?

What Price Freedom

What price freedom

What purpose or reason

What greatness achieve we

To be freed from our prison

What pressure release we

As we strive daily and plan

To obtain what is our right

Why want we just to be man

We only desire the freedom to live

To judge for ourselves

Those to whom allegiance we give

To yearn now no longer

From yesteryear's sorrows

To remove our past shackles

From our children's tomorrows

To live as we ought to

So proud upright and free

To have among all men full equality

Why deny this yet unto me

Why ask you our reasons

When you our woes brought

Thru slavery, torture and prisons

You my peoples sold and bought

You on your high throne

In gold splendour and lace

Built on the bleached bones

Of my Black beautiful race

You with your flag flying

In red with such pride

The red blood of my fathers

Who in your slavery suffered and died

You who did take fast

Their youth, country and name

Destroyed even their culture

Since the first day that you came

You who e'en still on my homeland abide

Whilst when we try to return home

You try to cast us aside

But yet you would still believe

The right is not ours to achieve

By whatever method now is quickest

That free men we may live

Well let's just stop and consider

The examples you have set

When your freedom was threatened

You fought and you're fighting yet

My peoples too long now to your policies have bowed

Ne'er seeing in fulfillment promised you avowed

So no longer can we wait

In peace while suffering shame

Whilst still you exploit us

While you still cause us pain

What price freedom what reason you ask

The price may be my life

The reason my life's only task

But this I do promise

And I'll keep it I vow

My peoples shall be FREE

By any method left now

You're Married...

You're married...

Aye, so it seems, and so am I but yet

How strange it matters not

Your eyes become a heavenly book

Your heart's voice speaks in every look you give

Ah... but sigh not my pretty one

The night's Moon follows close the setting Sun

To bid deeply to those that sigh with lonely tears

Hidden 'neath a sparkling eye...

A promise

Aye a promise of the rest of night

Of coming dawn of new days bright

Of things we once had dreamed like now

Of full and free and lasting love

Take not this tiny bit of thought

For slur or jest from one who oughtn't

But seek within your hidden fears

Re-visit all your hurts and pains

Then think of one who as thou art

Must live so near yet be apart

Away, away, away from life

Away from love next door to strife

Next door to all that casts one down

To e'er be trampled 'neath the ground

Of joyous pain or sorrow

And now it seems we two must part

And will not meet tomorrow.

A Song of Africans

Long before the days of England

'Way back in the days of yore

Back among, old Egypt's Pharaohs

Dignity the Black man wore

Like a cape full free and flowing

Like smoke on a breezy day

Thru his native homeland Africa

Spread freedoms message every way

Thru Mali and Songhai regions

Timbuktu to Egypt's door

From the southern cape so solemn

To the Mediterranean's shore

Freedom and the rights of living

Democracy in fullest style

Here the birthplace of civilization

Where the ancients resteth awhile

Here where Pharaohs in their glory

Would forever place to see

Egypt's wonders part of Africa

Part of our past histories

Here it was beside the Tigress

That the Gods once stopped to play

Here inside a dome caped city

Man and all life started they

Here where Christ so young would visit

Wrapped he yet in swaddling clothes

There to seek the sought for freedom

Where his life would be secure

On the banks where past meets present

Where the future full lies bare

Came so late the hate-filled Northman

Seeking to plunder not to share

Fourteen centuries long since Jesus

'Fore the Northern white man found

That a peoples rich and cultured

Lived in a land just Southern down

Came they then in ships with weapons

Only to find with grim surprise

Welcome warmth from all the natives

Friendly faces with smiling eyes

Savages they'd called these beings

Who had welcomed them as friend
Black and brown and red and yellow
Mixed they all as fellowmen
All the arts of their past cultures
So preserved and great was seen
That the Northern man in wonder
Stood aghast at what he'd seen
Stood and watched the labour given
Every day thru hot or cold
Saw the natives stand so tall still
Endurance strong in young and old
Saw the laws and institutions
Wherein each a lesson taught
Saw equality and justice
Each day democratically sought
While he looked and while he marveled
No fault herein could he find
Save the fact the God he worshiped
Was from theirs a different kind
On this basis he the Northman
Being blind to truth and fact
Condemned the roots of civilization
Condemned them cause their skin was black
In his haste and in his deep greed

He in cunning ways did lie

Promising new work as servants

If on him they would rely

In their trusting faithful manner

Many came to seek the world

Only fast to be held captive

Chained within a Slave-ships hold

Far away across the oceans

To a land where Indians died

Here by force to daily labour

Here to have all rights denied

Here to lose all touch of childhood

Here to lose all hope and pride

Here to live 'til death would free him

Thru centuries four condemned untried

Yet thru all his memories stay strong

And is song and story bold

He would keep the history of Africa

One day that truth to unfold

One day in the distant future

When the Northman became just

When they sought to find their origins

To Africa must they turn and trust

Then recalling all the years past

They would have to tell in truth

How they found a civilized culture

How from Africa came man's roots

They would dig and seek for answers

In the dirt the hills and caves

They would lastly take our writings

Told so often bold and brave

There within our past clear written

Mankind's origins clear would stand

Telling of the birth of life full

Bird, plant, animal and man

All the years lost in ignorance

Here the Northern man would see

Lay the hope of man's survival

Preserved here thru eternity

All the kings, the queens, the princes

All the poor and middle classed

All the infants taken forceful

Would be recognized at last

Then the Northman will stand slowly

As his past before him flies

As he finds that true civilization

He by mistake once despised

As today's technology quickens

As our past achievements show
Soon the Northern man'll admit it
In the past we it did know
As his head looks to the good earth
Where we at all sometimes gaze
The true meaning of equality
Will him then truly amaze
Then repentant tho he may be
He will not want to atone
For inside he still is thinking
He is right and he alone
He who o'er the years have taken
Fifty millions times by three
Children of the past from Africa
Peoples cultured strong and free
Peoples who have long long waited
In the hearts now of their young
To repay in fullest measure
For the past and all its wrong
Peoples who with patient hearts yet
In forgiving silence wait
Will not be content forever
To e'er see their rights abate
Peoples who in voice and manner

Tell the Northman one more time

Let us live in true full freedom

No longer try patience of mine

Give to me but freedom's banner

That my homelands I may see

Flying free thereo'er forever

That banner that belongs to me

Give my children for their future

But their rights to love and live

That in pride we once again all

May in our homelands freely live

Give us choice of friend and language

Let our voices shout in praise

That our song shall rise in valor

Telling of our past bleak days

"Give our young to live a reason

Give our old a rest full earned

Give to me again the Africa

Wherefrom all the world once learned

Then my past shall be a past thing

Then my blood shall no more boil

And I shall rest beneath my gravestone

Knowing it was worth my toil"

This Dreary Life is Filled So Full

This dreary life is filled so full
Of hatred hurt despair
That no longer feel I the pull
Of ambitiousness so dear
No longer can I stand and wait
For your laws to deal me justice
Living deep within your racist hate
While segregation and prejudice you practice
No longer will my people crawl
From pain, want, fear or danger
Nor stand like targets by the wall
There to die from shots or hunger
Your laws and Governments all stink
Corrupted by your fags and bigots
Your entire social system I think
Is suitable only to those high within it
No court will hold or give a damn
For they enjoy their persecutions
Long as it's a nigger there's no qualms
To o'erstep e'en their own limitations
Yet when reversed we see the stand
Then legal loopholes fast enter
To save from legalities any white man

If a black the suit doth enter
So how can we get justice done
Or e'en hope herein to find it
Death is our justice our only one
'Cause for us you whites don't give a shit

The Gods You Worship

The Gods you worship condemn you
The people you serve reject you
Those you govern are ashamed of you
The organizations of freedom ridicule you
And yet you cannot will not see
You close your eyes and ears
You pay no heed to my peoples' pleas
You continue to subjugate and corrupt
You continue to usurp and exploit
Hasn't 300 years been enough
Hasn't 300 years of slavery and pain
Brought enough pleasure to your sadistic brain
Shown you that our fight is still the same
Shown you that in subjection we won't remain
Hasn't it shown you we must be free
Of all your ties, your laws, your evil rules and men
Free to exist, to walk as free black men

Free to live to govern and exist

Free to be ourselves free you to resist

Yes free free free, free from you

Then take away England your chains

Take away all that even now remains

Take your colonials from our land

Let us be free ruled by our fellowman

Let us rejoice in valour firm and true

Let us enjoy again the pride our fathers knew

Before you made them slaves

Before you put them in their graves

Before you took them far from Africa

Before you on their blood did build

All your nation and you continue still

To use us as you did in years gone past

To build your world at our lives expense

To live with no thought of recompense

For the murder and the robbery you commit

Oh England the free world calls to you

The United Nations ridicule you too

The Red worlds speak of you with shame

Your own peoples turn against your name

Your past, present and your future too

Is red and red and white and blue

Is red with the blood you have shed
In the sale of my peoples which you led
Is white in streaks to show, to show
That your racist policies power
Tried the red blood to cover o'er
But topping all is that rich dark blue
Reminding you of the blacks you slew
Recalling how their African waters were
Recalling Caribbean seas e'en now
Recalling every place you stayed
Whilst you as the ruler of the sea
Your slave trips made
But still you will not set me free
This my land and country mine and me
This tiny atoll of an island small
Where we desire for our peoples all
Only freedom from your oppressing land
Only the right to live free with our brothers' man
Only to be masters of our own destiny
God damn you England — set us free
Take away your peoples and your flag
Your red white and blue of which you brag
And leave us that we may be free
Leave my black brothers, sisters and me
Leave us, leave us, leave us free.

I Believe in Life...

I believe the day will come when all shall end
I believe the time will be when each man's a friend
I believe... tho now I grieve... I believe
I believe one day the wrongs will all be right
I believe our eyes'll be blind to Black or White
I believe... tho now I grieve... I believe
I believe that you and I and all of mankind
Are searching deep
For a Peace
Which... Someday we'll find
I believe... Yes I believe
I believe that when the Summer comes
The Winter's snow it all shall end
I believe that in this World of woe
I'll live to love again... my friend
I believe... tho now I grieve... I believe
I believe that good things come
To those that wait
I believe that patience is the way
To change your fate
Everyday when I awake and see the light
I feel alive... because I'm right
For I believe that I'd live thru the night
To carry on... My struggling life...
Yes I believe... I believe...
I believe... I believe in life...

Of China

Of China I have often thought
Of its past pain and woes
Of the lies for which it fought
As from Demonocracy it did go
Of the truths it shares in other lands
Of the ways its peoples live
Of its aspirations and its plans
Of the lasting freedom it would give
To those whom I have met therefrom
Those who did the times survive
Tho all the wars and evils come
They did their lands revive
Those who would let me believe
That therein the demon lies
Which would destroy and let us grieve
If they could invade our skies
But I have found that they are too
A fast and noble race
Who tho they may not look like you
Deserve not to be disgraced
For in the time that they have had
To build a nation grand
They've built like builders going mad
To elevate their grand homeland.

There's a Story Being Told

There's a story being told

Of the voyages so bold

Which from my father's homeland you did sail

Of the rubies diamonds gold

Untold wealth you did behold

While you sought my peoples to enslave

Many ships did to there go

Of nations varied, we do know

So on you we will not all faults lay

Thus to statistics we did go

That our findings we could show

To remind you of the part you too did play

Every month our findings say

Six of your ships left our bays

Laden each with 300 freemen chained

To work and toil for you all day

On your plantations far away

'Cause your own of the toil complained

Beaten broken starved and pained

Many died but still you claimed

For 300 years those that did someway survive

Used as animals not men

You know why we know when

My peoples pride and courage did revive

Then the hand outstretched was clenched

The spoken word filled with hate full meant

And in surprise you ask why we so react

Wasn't food and shelter given

Enough for these savages you'd taken

What more pray desired now those Blacks?

Will You Spare a Moment

Will you spare but short a moment

As you pass my way along

Just to listen to my comment

As you pass by and are gone

Will you think back to the time when

You would not me look upon

For to do so 'twould remind you

That on me you'd heaped such wrong

Will you stop awhile and ponder

What I say — all of my words

And see if you can find one false

In that which you will have heard

Will you then lend me assistance

As you travel this life thru

Making race equality's resistance

A goal you'll stand against will you

Will you pause for but a moment

As my pains and hurts I bare

Or will you crush my every comment

And show the world you still don't care

You dear madam/sir in passing

Can but be one of two types

One who helped the slave in freeing

Or one who felt slavery was right

You can have but one choice stranger

A neutral stance no longer take

For neutrals serves but to endanger

Each step we do for freedom make

For we in past lives have believed true

Lived in shame 'cause slaves we'd been

Taught to respect those like you

Who longed to push us down again

But alas our eyes have opened

We the wretched the unfree

We who were the peoples stolen

Away from family, home, country

We who long have silent suffered

Heaping on ourselves the blame

Slaves we were and as slaves we offered

Small resistance — accepting shame

Now we know you were the owners

You the slaver, master, thief

You who stole must bear the onus

Bear the rightful shame and grief

You must now be made to look back

At the wrongs you did commit

'Til you start to respect the man Black

And you will your pasts admit

Until then dear sir or madam

On your conscience this may you keep

I lay each night in mental comfort

Whilst your past doth haunt your sleep

Thank you for your pause and moment

And for looking back awhile

At the shame brought by your peoples

Brought to you by a slave's grandchild

Oh You Dumb Bigoted Fiend

Oh you dumb bigoted fiend

Know you not what freedom means

To each person no matter what their colour be

You who want the best from life

You took my fathers' home and life

And e'en yet you try to make a slave of me

When my people freedom sought

Like property which could be bought

On your throne you did their value in coins figure

'Til at length your clerks arrived

At a figure when unmultiplied

Paid to the owners "1/2 cent for each Nigger"

Over 300 years as slaves

Over 130 million in their graves

The land and wealth of our fathers now you own

Yet you still dare to look up high

Talk of a just God in the sky

And yet quibble when we seek to lead our own

But we've served our days as slaves

Now we demand on our fathers' graves

That no longer will you hold us in your hands

So if together we cannot live

Our complete freedom you won't give

Then get out now from all our rich Black lands

Give us the lands which you did take

When John Hawkins slaves of us did make

Which for this act by knighthood

you honoured him grand

Be our land now large or small

Rich or poor give them back all

That your damned soul may know peace

O England

Internal Self Government... We Really Need It

We really need it

There's got to be some changes made around here

We come home — our wives can't cook

Children can't go to school with no books

I.S.G. we really need it

There's got to be some changes made around here

Here's your grip — there's the door

Tell us what are you waiting for

I.S.G. we really need it

There's got to be some changes made around here

We work like slaves — night and day

All we get is a semi-slave pay

I.S.G. we really need it

There's got to be some changes made around here

We vote our peoples — to keep us free

Then find they can't speak in the Assembly

I.S.G. we really need it

There's got to be some changes made around here

300 years we been true to the Crown

Now it seems to Yanks we gonna be let down

I.S.G. we really need it

There's got to be some changes made around here

We've waited and worked — so long you see

But only I.S.G. can set us free

I.S.G. we really need it

There's got to be some changes made around here

I.S.G. — I.S.G. is what we need to be free

I.S.G. we really need it

There's gonna be a lot of changes made around here

Note: Cayman I.S.G. (1966) election song

My Father Was a Poor Man

My father was a poor man

The son of your past slave

My mother too did bend her back

Whilst a child your whip to brave

In silence they have paid the price

For being proud and black

You've tortured them and them chastised

Still they ne'er paid you back

But unbeknown to you that time

They too were raising young

Who freedom would seek to find

Fore their early strength was gone

Children of slaves who'd seen the life

You'd dished out to their peoples

Who'd been refused an entrance in

Your church with white tall steeple

Children whose minds would not accept

The ways their parents live

Children who know that violence

Could take what you won't give

Children who are not afraid

To stop their lives in youth

If it will but serve instead

To show the world the truth

I am one of those children

Upon my back you'll find

The marks of whips you used again

Once too oft on backs like mine

In sleep you lay when in I came

So cozy in beds of white

No thought that your age old game

Would be reversed tonight

You pray to your white God above

Whom you worship once a week

While laws to stay learning of his love

Is all you e'er to me speak

Then cast your frightened eyes so red

Upon me your "damn black slave"

And take the visions of my four hundred years

Of suffering to your grave

Be Wary of the Things in Life

Be wary of the things you see in life

They may not be as you perceive

Beware of those in grips of hardships or strife

It may be only a front you to deceive

Walk not where your eyes would lead you

Follow not the ways of a helping plan

Strive to control the mass or a few

But thru all beware of man

Beware of all that you are hearing

Your young ears have no experience with lies

Beware of all those with you pleading

Why waste time on their feeble cries

Stay away from the sorrows all around you

Strive to better yourself as you can

Let them suffer or die but I warn you

Don't waste time beware of man

We are the older people who speak

We who have seen and heard it all past

We didn't survive by assisting the weak

And you won't if your finances don't last

For thru the years of our living

We have scraped and gained full elation

But it came by our saving not giving

Nor being concerned by mere inflation

Yes our lives are examples for you all

To follow fast therein is our plan

To come only if the bugles of war call

And to ever beware beware

Beware of the poor man

'Tis Been a Long Long Time Ago

'Tis been a long long time ago

Since first you saw my face

Since Africa you did go to

And enslaved the free black race

'Tis been so many years ago

That you have it seems forgot

That we were free and this we know

It was our rightful lot

We've suffered now four hundred years

In death and hurt and pain

As slaves as animals in fear

In humility disgrace and shame

We've bled to satisfy your lust

For land and gold and wealth

We've built up all your nothingness

Taken care of your ill health

We've been a servant such as man

Could never hope to find

Without a word or thought again

Of hate given by your race to mine

But then alas the saying old

Holds true and now applies

You never miss the water's flow

Until the well runs dry

That well was slavery and the slave

Was water flowing free

It mattered not how many killed

You could always replace me

For it seems you said to use your quote

That in Africa of blacks there be

No end to them, their choice, their kind

End of quote — now here stands me

I am the first and thus the last

I stand for all wrongs heaped

I call for restitution for the past

For payment for our labours cheap

I call for full free equal rights

For each black woman child and man

You know our strength unity and might

Can destroy your slave built land.

See the Seagulls

See the Seagulls

See the grey and black and white

See the flutterings of the wings

As they soar in blissful flight

See the beaks now open wide

As they reach to grasp therein

The free food that they do find

As it is thrown out unto them

Far away from land they be

Out here o'er waters calm

From where doth their food it come

Flying there from outstretched arm

'Tis a tiny child below

On the deck of some ship huge

Which in playful wish doth throw

O'er the side bits of refuse

That small arm outstretched you see

Is trying hard to reach above

To the Seagulls he can see

Filling his tiny heart with love

All too soon will come the day

When the Seagulls will not fly

When the child no more will stay

Nor to feed those Seagulls try

But there'll come each time anew

Another boat, Seagull and child

And the Seagull 'twill look anew

To take food and recreate smiles.

West Point Grey...

Moon looking over the waters

Looking o'er West Point Grey

Tell me what you're thinking

In your melancholy way

As the lights all twinkle

Like stars so high above

You shine on the city sleeping

From your eternal place above

You make for all who watch you

A path upon the waves

You create desire to walk the path

And join you watching there

Yet Moon so bright and yellow

So soft yet distant too

You with your beams so mellow

Are you ever really blue

When you go from my eyes

To a place I do not know

When you seem to leave the skies

Moon where do you go

The tall majestic mountains

The city hills and plains

All seem so dark and dreary

Whenever you are shining

And far tho you may wander

On your journeys this World wide

You'll always be a memory

Which I'll ponder when you hide.

Other Collections by This Author:

A Poet's Ebb And Flow

... and Touches Of Nature

In The Middle of Believe There's A Lie

Inside A Heart

Legends, Lives & Loves Along the Inside Passage

Love... Life's Illusive Zenith

Love's Reflections

Love's Refuge and Sonnets

Only Children Of The Universe Are We

Step Scenes Of Life

That We Too Free May Live

~ ~

For more information go to:

w w w . d n c s i t e . c a

~ ~